Selling with Integrity

Sell Like Jesus

The Perfect Role Model!

(Sell with Christ-like Excellence)

Gerard Assey

Selling with Integrity

Sell Like Jesus

The Perfect Role Model!

By

Gerard Assey

Published by:
Gerard Assey
19/18, Palli Arasan Street
Anna Nagar East
Chennai - 600 102

ISBN: 978-93-92492-82-2

(Image courtesy by: https://www.freepik.com-Thank You)

Table of Contents

Preface

In a world where selling can sometimes be associated with self-interest and manipulation, there is a dire need for a transformative approach that reflects genuine care, integrity, and compassion. As sales professionals, we are called to be more than just sellers of products or services; we are called to be ambassadors of positive change.

In this book, '**Selling with Integrity: Sell Like Jesus -The Perfect Role Model!'** we embark on a journey of rediscovery, drawing inspiration from the life and teachings of the ultimate Role Model - Jesus Christ. Just as Jesus touched the lives of countless individuals through love, empathy, and servant leadership, we too can create meaningful connections with our customers, transforming our sales approach into a testimony of faith, trust, and integrity.

Throughout these pages, we will explore the eight fundamental steps of selling, each viewed through the lens of biblical principles and Jesus' example. From prospecting with compassion to providing exceptional customer service with unwavering love, we will uncover how aligning our actions with godly virtues elevates not only our sales performance but also our impact on the lives of those we serve.

Let us set aside conventional sales techniques and embrace the timeless wisdom of Jesus - the perfect Role Model in Sales. May this journey empower us to make a difference in the world, one customer at a time, as we emulate the heart of Jesus in every interaction and transaction.

May this book inspire you to embark on a new and transformative chapter in your sales career, where selling becomes a platform for bringing hope, joy, and God's love into the lives of others. Together, let us walk in the footsteps of Jesus, as we sell with integrity, compassion, and purpose.

Go Ahead! Sell with Christ-like Excellence!

Why is it Important for Sales Professionals to follow JESUS as the Role Model when Selling?

Following Jesus as the role model is essential for sales professionals because it aligns their actions and values with Godly principles. Emulating Jesus in selling can lead to various benefits for both the salesperson and the customers. Here are some specific examples of how following Jesus as the role model can help sales professionals:

1. **Compassionate Outreach and Respect:** Sales professionals who follow Jesus' approach of compassionate outreach and respect can build stronger connections with potential customers. By genuinely caring for customers' needs and treating them with respect, sales professionals foster trust and openness.
   Biblical Perspective: Jesus' interaction with the Samaritan woman (John 4:4-26) demonstrates how approaching others with compassion and respect can lead to life-changing encounters.
2. **Integrity and Honesty:** Jesus prioritized honesty and integrity in His teachings and actions. Sales professionals who embrace these qualities gain credibility with customers and foster long-term relationships based on trust.
   Biblical Perspective: Jesus' commitment to truthfulness, even when faced with challenges

(John 8:1-11), exemplifies the importance of integrity in sales.

3. **Empathy and Understanding:** Sales professionals who practice empathy, like Jesus did, can uncover customers' true needs and concerns. By understanding customers' pain points, sales professionals can offer tailored solutions and build deeper connections.
   Biblical Perspective: Jesus' compassion for the hungry crowd (Matthew 14:13-21) exemplifies the power of empathy in meeting people's needs.
4. **Servant Leadership:** Emulating Jesus' servant leadership approach helps sales professionals prioritize the customers' well-being above personal gain. By serving customers with genuine care, sales professionals can create positive experiences and lasting loyalty.
   Biblical Perspective: Jesus' washing of the disciples' feet (John 13:1-17) exemplifies servant leadership and selflessness.
5. **Patience and Grace in Handling Objections:** Sales professionals, who handle objections with patience and grace, like Jesus did with His disciples, can turn resistance into opportunities for meaningful dialogue and understanding.
   Biblical Perspective: Jesus' patient response to Thomas' doubts (John 20:24-29) demonstrates the importance of addressing objections with grace.
6. **Faithfulness and Love in Customer Service:** Sales professionals who show

faithfulness and love in customer service, akin to Jesus' commitment to His disciples, create strong relationships that result in customer retention and referrals.

Biblical Perspective: Jesus' post-resurrection appearances to His disciples (John 21:15-19) exemplify faithfulness and love in nurturing relationships.

By following Jesus as the role model, sales professionals can build a reputation of integrity, compassion, and servant leadership, which can lead to enhanced customer trust, loyalty, and ultimately, business success. Moreover, aligning their sales practices with Godly principles brings a sense of purpose and fulfillment to their profession, as they seek to serve and impact others positively.

Sales Professionals using JESUS as the Role Model to SELL- the Key Challenges One can Face in this World, and How to Overcome Them

As a Sales Professional using Jesus as the Role Model, you may encounter various challenges in the world of selling. By drawing inspiration from Jesus' teachings and example, you can navigate these challenges with integrity, love, and wisdom. Here are some key challenges and how to handle them:

1. **Rejection and Resistance:** Sales professionals often face rejection and resistance from potential customers. Emulate Jesus' perseverance and grace in handling rejection by not taking it personally and continuing to show genuine care.
   Biblical Perspective: Jesus faced rejection and opposition throughout His ministry, yet He remained steadfast in His mission to share God's love and truth.
2. **Pressure to Prioritize Profits Over People:** In a competitive sales environment, there might be pressure to prioritize profits over the well-being of customers. Follow Jesus' example of prioritizing people's needs and serving them with compassion.
   Biblical Perspective: Jesus emphasized the importance of serving others selflessly, even when it meant personal sacrifice (Matthew 20:28).
3. **Dealing with Unethical Practices:** Sales professionals might encounter situations

where they are tempted to engage in unethical practices to achieve targets. Stay true to Jesus' teachings of honesty and integrity, even in challenging situations.
Biblical Perspective: Jesus emphasized the importance of honesty and integrity in all dealings (Matthew 5:37).

4. **Handling Difficult Customers:** Encountering difficult customers can be challenging. Follow Jesus' example of patience and understanding, seeking to resolve conflicts with grace and empathy.
   Biblical Perspective: Jesus showed patience and compassion to those who were troubled or confrontational (Matthew 9:20-22, Mark 5:25-34).
5. **Balancing Work and Personal Life:** Sales professionals often face the challenge of maintaining a healthy work-life balance. Follow Jesus' example of seeking moments of solitude and prayer for renewal and guidance.
   Biblical Perspective: Jesus often withdrew to quiet places to pray and recharge (Luke 5:16).
6. **Facing Competition and Comparison:** In a competitive sales environment, sales professionals may feel the pressure to compare themselves to others. Embrace Jesus' teaching on individual uniqueness and focus on personal growth and improvement.
   Biblical Perspective: Jesus reminded Peter not to compare his journey with others but to focus on following Him (John 21:21-22).
7. **Ethical Dilemmas and Decision-making:** Sales professionals may encounter ethical dilemmas that require making tough decisions.

Seek wisdom and guidance from Jesus' teachings and prioritize moral integrity.

Biblical Perspective: Jesus' teachings emphasized doing what is right, even when faced with difficult choices (Matthew 5:8).

By using Jesus as the Role Model in selling, you can navigate these challenges with grace, integrity, and love. Draw inspiration from His teachings and example to prioritize serving others, practicing empathy, and upholding Godly principles in all aspects of your sales journey. Remember, following Jesus' footsteps will not only make you a successful sales professional but also a positive influence in the lives of those you serve.

The Key Skills, Traits, and Attributes of Sales Professional that use JESUS as the Role Model when Selling

Sales professionals who use Jesus as the Role Model exhibit specific skills, traits, and attributes that align with biblical principles. Here are some key qualities:

1. **Compassion and Empathy:** Emulating Jesus' compassion and empathy helps sales professionals understand customers' needs and concerns genuinely.
   Biblical Perspective: Jesus showed compassion to the hungry crowd and healed the sick (Matthew 14:14, Luke 4:40).
2. **Integrity and Honesty:** Following Jesus' example of honesty and integrity builds trust with customers.
   Biblical Perspective: Jesus emphasized the importance of truthfulness in His teachings (John 8:32).
3. **Patience and Grace:** Sales professionals who demonstrate patience and grace can handle objections and challenges with understanding.
   Biblical Perspective: Jesus displayed patience with His disciples and extended grace to those in need (Matthew 17:17, Luke 7:36-50).
4. **Servant Leadership:** Embracing servant leadership, like Jesus, enables sales professionals to prioritize the well-being of customers over personal gain.

Biblical Perspective: Jesus washed His disciples' feet, exemplifying servant leadership (John 13:4-5).

5. **Effective Communication:** Following Jesus' example of effective communication helps sales professionals connect with customers on a deeper level.
   Biblical Perspective: Jesus used parables and clear teachings to convey His message to diverse audiences (Matthew 13:34, Luke 19:11-27).
6. **Genuine Care for Customers:** Sales professionals who genuinely care for customers build strong and lasting relationships.
   Biblical Perspective: Jesus' love for His disciples and followers reflects genuine care and concern (John 13:1, John 15:9-17).
7. **Diligence and Wisdom:** Emulating Jesus' diligence and wisdom helps sales professionals prepare and plan for successful engagements.
   Biblical Perspective: Jesus spent time in prayer and solitude to seek God's guidance (Luke 6:12).
8. **Resilience and Perseverance:** Following Jesus' example of resilience helps sales professionals bounce back from setbacks and stay committed to their mission.
   Biblical Perspective: Jesus endured challenges and persecution throughout His ministry (Mark 14:50, Luke 23:33-34).
9. **Selflessness and Sacrifice:** Sales professionals who prioritize others' needs over

their own demonstrate selflessness and sacrifice.
Biblical Perspective: Jesus willingly sacrificed Himself for the salvation of humanity (John 10:17-18, Philippians 2:5-8).

10. **Faith and Trust in God:** Embracing faith and trust in God, as Jesus did, gives sales professionals confidence in uncertain situations.
Biblical Perspective: Jesus' reliance on His Father's will guided His actions (John 5:30, Luke 22:42).

By embodying these skills, traits, and attributes, sales professionals can create meaningful connections with customers and conduct their work with a sense of purpose, reflecting Jesus' teachings of love, service, and integrity.

Why is the Right Attitude and Mindset so Very Important for a Sales Professional

The right attitude and mindset are crucial for a Sales Professional using Jesus as the Role Model because they shape how the salesperson approaches their work and interacts with customers. A positive and Christ-like mindset can lead to a more impactful and authentic selling experience. Here are some examples from a biblical context to illustrate the importance of the right attitude and mindset:

- ✓ **Humility and Servant hood:** Having a humble attitude, just like Jesus, allows the sales professional to prioritize serving customers' needs above personal achievements. Jesus, despite being the Son of God, humbled Himself to serve others, even washing His disciples' feet (John 13:4-5).
- ✓ **Love and Compassion:** Emulating Jesus' love and compassion helps the sales professional genuinely care for their customers. When Jesus encountered the crowd, He had compassion on them and taught them many things (Mark 6:34).
- ✓ **Patience and Understanding:** A patient and understanding attitude enables the sales professional to empathize with customers' concerns and address objections thoughtfully. Jesus displayed patience with His disciples, often explaining His teachings and parables to ensure their understanding (Mark 4:34).

- ✓ **Resilience and Perseverance:** Following Jesus' example of resilience helps the sales professional overcome rejections and setbacks with a determined spirit. Despite facing opposition and challenges, Jesus remained steadfast in His mission to spread God's message (Luke 9:51).
- ✓ **Faith and Trust in God's Plan:** Having faith and trusting in God's plan gives the sales professional confidence in uncertain situations. Jesus demonstrated unwavering faith in God, even during His crucifixion, saying, "Father, into your hands, I commit my spirit" (Luke 23:46).
- ✓ **Integrity and Honesty:** Adopting Jesus' commitment to truthfulness and integrity fosters trust with customers. Jesus consistently spoke the truth and lived by example, stating, "I am the way, and the truth, and the life" (John 14:6).
- ✓ **Gratitude and Thankfulness:** A mindset of gratitude helps the sales professional appreciate and acknowledge customers' support and trust. Jesus often expressed thankfulness to God for His provision and blessings (Matthew 15:36).
- ✓ **Optimism and Positivity:** Maintaining a positive outlook allows the sales professional to inspire and uplift customers. Jesus encouraged His disciples with hopeful messages, assuring them of His presence even after His departure (John 14:1-3).

By cultivating these attitudes and mindsets, the Sales Professional using Jesus as the Role Model can create a sales approach rooted in love, service, and authenticity. Such an approach not only benefits the salesperson but also fosters meaningful relationships with customers, reflecting Jesus' teachings of grace, compassion, and selflessness.

Introduction to the Key Steps in Selling: Jesus-The Ultimate Role Model in Sales

In the world of sales, success is often defined by numbers, targets, and profits. However, at the core of every salesperson's journey lies the quest for meaningful connections, genuine relationships, and a desire to make a positive impact on the lives of others. In this chapter, we delve into the significance of Jesus as the ultimate role model in sales, drawing inspiration from His life and teachings to set a firm foundation for applying biblical principles in the sales process.

The Significance of Jesus as the Perfect Sales Role Model: Jesus' life was marked by compassion, empathy, wisdom, and servant leadership. He walked on this earth with a profound purpose - to seek and save the lost, heal the brokenhearted, and serve those in need. His teachings transcended societal norms, touching the hearts of individuals from all walks of life. As we explore Jesus' significance as a sales role model, we discover that successful selling is not solely about closing deals but about understanding, connecting, and serving people genuinely.

Setting the Foundation for Applying Biblical Principles to the Sales Process: The foundation of our sales journey lies in aligning our values and actions with the timeless truths found in the Bible. Jesus' teachings emphasize love, honesty, integrity, humility, and putting others' needs before our own. By embracing these Godly principles, we can elevate the sales process to one that fosters trust, respect, and long-lasting relationships with customers.

Applying the Godly Principle - Love and Authenticity: One of the key principles that we can apply from Jesus' example is love and authenticity. Jesus approached people with genuine care and concern, reflecting His love for humanity. In the same way, as sales professionals, we can learn to approach our customers with a sincere desire to understand their needs and provide tailored solutions.

Example: Imagine a salesperson in a car dealership interacting with a potential customer who is indecisive about purchasing a car. Instead of pressuring the customer into making a quick decision, the salesperson takes the time to listen to their preferences and requirements. With authentic care, the salesperson recommends a vehicle that aligns with the customer's needs, even if it means suggesting a lower-priced option. The customer appreciates the salesperson's honesty and feels valued, leading to a deeper level of trust.

Benefits to the Customer: By applying the Godly principle of love and authenticity, the salesperson not only earns the customer's trust but also ensures that the customer receives a product that truly meets their needs. This authentic approach builds a strong foundation for a lasting relationship, encouraging the customer to return for future purchases and refer friends and family to the dealership.

In this introduction, we invite sales professionals to embark on a transformative journey of emulating Jesus' example in their sales approach. By understanding the significance of Jesus as the perfect role model and setting a foundation based on biblical principles, we can elevate our selling experience to one that is purposeful, impactful, and guided by Godly values.

Prospecting and Lead Generation: Learning from Jesus' Approach

The first step in the sales process, Prospecting and Lead Generation, sets the groundwork for successful interactions with potential customers. In this step, we can draw inspiration from Jesus' approach to reaching out to diverse individuals with compassion and understanding.

Jesus' Compassionate Outreach to Diverse Individuals: Throughout His earthly ministry, Jesus demonstrated deep compassion for people from all walks of life. He reached out to the marginalized, the sick, the outcasts, and the wealthy alike, showing no partiality or discrimination. Jesus' heart for the lost and His desire to offer hope and healing serve as a powerful model for sales professionals as they embark on prospecting and lead generation.

Finding Inspiration in Jesus' Methods of Engaging Potential Customers: Jesus engaged potential followers through meaningful interactions, meeting them where they were and addressing their specific needs. He understood the unique circumstances and pain points of individuals and offered genuine solutions to their problems. His approach was not forceful or manipulative but rooted in authentic care and empathy.

Applying the Godly Principle - Compassion and Understanding: As sales professionals, we can apply the Godly principle of compassion and understanding in our prospecting efforts. Rather than viewing potential customers solely as leads or opportunities for sales, we seek to empathize with their situations, challenges, and desires. We approach them with genuine care, seeking to build connections that go beyond transactional interactions.

Example: Consider a salesperson working for a financial advisory firm. Instead of cold-calling a list of potential clients with a scripted sales pitch, the salesperson takes a compassionate approach. They research the individuals' financial circumstances and concerns and reach out with personalized messages addressing their specific needs. The salesperson expresses empathy, understanding the stress that financial decisions can bring, and offers to provide guidance and solutions to help the clients achieve their financial goals.

Benefits to the Customer: By applying the Godly principle of compassion and understanding, the salesperson demonstrates care and concern for the customer's well-being. This authentic approach builds trust and credibility, making the potential customer more receptive to the salesperson's guidance and recommendations. The customer feels valued and heard, fostering a deeper connection that can lead to a long-term and mutually beneficial relationship.

Relevant Bible Verses:

Matthew 9:35-36 - *"Jesus went through all the towns and villages, teaching in their synagogues, proclaiming the good news of the kingdom and healing every disease and sickness. When he saw the crowds, he had compassion on them because they were harassed and helpless, like sheep without a shepherd."*

Application of the Principle: Just as Jesus had compassion on the crowds, we, too, approach potential customers with empathy and compassion, recognizing their needs and offering genuine solutions.

Conclusion: In the prospecting and lead generation step, sales professionals can learn from Jesus' approach of compassionate outreach and meaningful engagement. By applying the Godly principle of compassion and understanding, we elevate our prospecting efforts to a level of authentic care, fostering trust and building lasting relationships with potential customers.

Preparing and Planning: Drawing Wisdom from Jesus' Diligence

The step of preparing and planning is crucial in the sales process as it sets the stage for successful engagements with customers. In this step, we can draw wisdom from Jesus' example of prayerful preparation for His ministry and apply diligence and wisdom in our sales approach.

Learning from Jesus' Prayerful Preparation for Ministry: Before embarking on His public ministry, Jesus spent significant time in prayer and communion with God the Father. He sought divine guidance and wisdom, aligning His actions with God's will. Jesus understood the importance of seeking spiritual preparation before carrying out His earthly mission, and His reliance on God's wisdom serves as a powerful lesson for sales professionals.

Applying Diligence and Wisdom in Preparing for Sales Engagements: Just as Jesus prepared diligently for His ministry, sales professionals should apply the same diligence and wisdom in preparing for sales engagements. This includes researching potential clients, understanding their specific needs and pain points, and tailoring our approach to meet their requirements. Diligent preparation enables us to deliver personalized and relevant solutions, increasing the likelihood of successful outcomes.

Applying the Godly Principle - Prayerful Preparation and Diligence: The Godly principle we can apply in this step is the combination of prayerful preparation and diligence. Just as Jesus sought guidance from God before embarking on His ministry, we can seek wisdom and direction through prayer, asking for insight and discernment in our sales endeavors. Additionally, applying diligence and investing time and effort in research and preparation ensures that we approach each sales engagement with professionalism and competence.

Example: Suppose a salesperson is preparing to pitch a product to a potential client. Instead of relying solely on a generic presentation, the salesperson begins with prayer, seeking God's wisdom and guidance for the upcoming meeting. They conduct thorough research on the client's industry, challenges, and competitors to understand the specific needs and pain points. Armed with this knowledge, the salesperson tailors their presentation to address the client's unique concerns and showcase how the product can provide meaningful solutions.

Benefits to the Customer: By applying the Godly principle of prayerful preparation and diligence, the salesperson demonstrates a genuine interest in the customer's needs. The personalized approach shows that the salesperson values the client's time and investment, leading to a more engaging and fruitful conversation. The customer feels understood and appreciated, increasing their confidence in the salesperson's ability to provide valuable solutions.

Relevant Bible Verses:

Luke 6:12-13 - *"One of those days Jesus went out to a mountainside to pray, and spent the night praying to God. When morning came, he called his disciples to him and chose twelve of them..."*

Application of the Principle: Just as Jesus spent time in prayerful preparation before choosing His disciples, we can seek God's wisdom and guidance through prayer as we prepare for sales engagements, ensuring we approach them with purpose and direction.

Conclusion: In the preparing and planning step, sales professionals can draw wisdom from Jesus' diligent preparation for His ministry. By applying the Godly principle of prayerful preparation and diligence, we elevate our sales approach to one that is grounded in spiritual guidance and tailored to meet the unique needs of our customers. This thoughtful preparation leads to more meaningful and successful sales interactions.

Approaching the Customer: Emulating Jesus' Love and Respect

Approaching the customer is a pivotal moment in the sales process, as it sets the tone for the entire interaction. By emulating Jesus' example of love and respect in His interactions with diverse individuals, sales professionals can build meaningful connections and foster trust with their customers.

Jesus' Interactions with Different Individuals and Showing Genuine Care: Throughout His earthly ministry, Jesus interacted with people from various backgrounds, cultures, and social statuses. He treated each individual with genuine care, recognizing their intrinsic value and worth. Jesus broke societal norms by engaging with outcasts, demonstrating compassion to the hurting, and respecting everyone, regardless of their position in society.

Applying Love and Respect in Approaching Customers for Meaningful Connections: As sales professionals, we can apply the Godly principle of love and respect when approaching customers. Instead of viewing them as merely potential buyers, we seek to understand them as unique individuals with their own needs, desires, and challenges. Approaching customers with a heart of love and respect creates a welcoming atmosphere for open and honest communication.

Applying the Godly Principle - Love and Respect: The Godly principle to apply in this step is love and respect, which we can exemplify in our interactions with customers. Just as Jesus loved and respected everyone He encountered, regardless of their background, we too can approach our customers with genuine care and consideration.

Example: Suppose a salesperson is approaching a potential customer who has expressed interest in a new home security system. Instead of rushing to present the product's features, the salesperson takes the time to listen to the customer's concerns and fears about home safety. They approach the customer with empathy, recognizing the importance of feeling secure in their own home. The salesperson then tailors their presentation to address the specific security needs of the customer's household.

Benefits to the Customer: By applying the Godly principle of love and respect, the salesperson creates a safe and caring environment for the customer. The customer feels valued and understood, and their concerns are acknowledged with empathy. This approach fosters trust and confidence in the salesperson's recommendations, increasing the likelihood of a positive sales outcome.

Relevant Bible Verses:

Mark 10:13-16 - *"People were bringing little children to Jesus for him to place his hands on them, but the disciples rebuked them. When Jesus saw this, he was indignant. He said to them, 'Let the little children come to me, and do not hinder them, for the kingdom of God belongs to such as these. Truly I tell you, anyone who will not receive the kingdom of God like a little child will never enter it.' And he took the children in his arms, placed his hands on them, and blessed them."*

Application of the Principle: Just as Jesus welcomed and blessed the little children, we can approach our customers with love and respect, valuing them as unique individuals and understanding their needs.

Conclusion: Approaching the customer with Jesus' example of love and respect transforms the sales interaction into a meaningful connection. By applying the Godly principle of love and respect, sales professionals create an environment of empathy and understanding, fostering trust and building lasting relationships with customers. This approach serves as the foundation for authentic and successful sales engagements.

Uncovering Needs and Pain: Practicing Compassion Like Jesus

The step of uncovering needs and pain is a critical aspect of the sales process, as it allows sales professionals to understand the challenges, needs and desires of their customers. By practicing compassion like Jesus, sales professionals can demonstrate genuine care and empathy, leading to meaningful solutions that address customers' pain points.

Jesus' Empathy in Understanding People's Needs and Struggles: Throughout His ministry, Jesus displayed extraordinary empathy and understanding of people's needs and struggles. He healed the sick, comforted the grieving, and addressed the spiritual and emotional needs of those He encountered. Jesus went beyond surface-level interactions, delving into the hearts of individuals to comprehend their deepest desires and longings.

Demonstrating Compassion to Identify Customers' Pain Points and Provide Solutions: As sales professionals, we can follow Jesus' example of compassion to uncover the pain points and needs of our customers. Instead of solely focusing on selling products or services, we take the time to listen attentively to our customers' concerns and challenges. We seek to comprehend not just their immediate requirements but also the underlying emotions and aspirations that drive their decision-making.

Applying the Godly Principle - Compassion: The Godly principle to apply in this step is compassion. Just as Jesus empathized with the struggles and pain of those He encountered, we too can approach our customers with a heart of compassion and understanding.

Example: Suppose a salesperson is speaking with a small business owner who is experiencing financial difficulties due to the COVID-19 pandemic. Instead of pushing a standard package of products, the salesperson practices compassion by asking open-ended questions to understand the specific challenges the business is facing. The salesperson listens carefully to the owner's concerns about staying afloat, keeping employees on payroll, and maintaining customer relationships amid uncertainty.

Benefits to the Customer: By applying the Godly principle of compassion, the salesperson demonstrates genuine care for the customer's well-being. The customer feels heard and valued, knowing that the salesperson is not simply looking to make a sale but to provide meaningful solutions. The salesperson can then offer tailored products or services that address the customer's unique pain points, offering genuine support during challenging times.

Relevant Bible Verses:

Matthew 14:14 - *"When Jesus landed and saw a large crowd, he had compassion on them and healed their sick."*

Application of the Principle: Just as Jesus had compassion on the large crowd and healed their sick, we can approach our customers with compassion, seeking to understand their needs and offering solutions to bring healing and relief.

Conclusion: Practicing compassion like Jesus in uncovering needs and pain enables sales professionals to build meaningful connections with customers. By applying the Godly principle of compassion, sales professionals demonstrate genuine care and empathy, leading to tailored solutions that address customers' pain points. This approach fosters trust and strengthens the relationship between the salesperson and the customer, creating a foundation for successful sales engagements.

Proving Value: Honesty and Integrity - The Jesus Way

In the step of proving value, sales professionals aim to demonstrate the worth and benefits of their products or services to customers. Embracing honesty and integrity, following the example set by Jesus, becomes crucial in this process to build credibility and trust.

Jesus' Truthful Teachings and the Importance of Honesty in Sales: Throughout His ministry, Jesus consistently emphasized the value of truthfulness and honesty. His teachings centered on integrity, love, and transparency, encouraging His followers to speak the truth and act with integrity. Jesus' unwavering commitment to the truth reflects the importance of these principles in every aspect of life, including sales.

Building Credibility by Proving Value with Integrity in Selling: Sales professionals can apply the Godly principles of honesty and integrity in proving the value of their products or services. This involves being transparent about the features and benefits of what they offer and refraining from misleading or exaggerating claims. By communicating honestly and genuinely with customers, sales professionals build credibility, which is essential for a lasting and fruitful business relationship.

Applying the Godly Principle - Honesty and Integrity: The Godly principle of honesty and integrity is the cornerstone of proving value handling. As Jesus exemplified, sales professionals must be truthful in their dealings, offering products or services that genuinely meet the customers' needs and provide tangible value.

Example: Imagine a salesperson selling nutritional supplements. Instead of making exaggerated claims about the products' effects, the salesperson focuses on educating the customer about the ingredients, scientific research, and potential benefits. The salesperson provides honest information about the supplements' limitations and encourages the customer to consult with their healthcare professional before making a decision.

Benefits to the Customer: By applying the Godly principle of honesty and integrity, the salesperson fosters trust and credibility with the customer. The customer appreciates the transparent and truthful approach, knowing that the salesperson has their best interests at heart. As a result, the customer can make an informed decision based on the value and benefits the products genuinely offer.

Relevant Bible Verses:

Proverbs 12:22 - *"The Lord detests lying lips, but he delights in people who are trustworthy."*

Application of the Principle: Just as the Lord delights in people who are trustworthy, sales professionals can apply honesty and integrity in their approach to proving value. By upholding the truth and demonstrating transparency, sales professionals honor God's desire for honesty in all aspects of life.

Conclusion: In proving value handling, sales professionals can learn from Jesus' example of honesty and integrity. By applying the Godly principle of truthfulness in their interactions with customers, sales professionals build credibility and trust. Embracing the Jesus way of honesty ensures that the value they offer is grounded in integrity, fostering lasting and meaningful relationships with customers.

Removing Objections/Concerns: Patience and Grace - Jesus' Approach

The step of removing objections and concerns is a crucial part of the sales process, as it allows sales professionals to address any hesitations or doubts that potential customers may have. Learning from Jesus' patient and gracious responses to skepticism and doubts, sales professionals can handle objections with understanding and build trust with their customers.

Learning from Jesus' Patient Responses to Skepticism and Doubts: Throughout His ministry, Jesus encountered skepticism and doubts from various individuals, including His disciples and the religious leaders. Yet, Jesus responded with patience and understanding, taking the time to address their concerns and provide reassurance. His unwavering love and grace allowed Him to engage in meaningful dialogue and fostered an atmosphere of trust.

Handling Objections with Grace to Overcome Resistance and Build Trust: Sales professionals can apply the Godly principles of patience and grace when handling objections and concerns. Instead of becoming defensive or dismissive, they approach objections with understanding and empathy. By responding with patience, sales professionals show their customers that they value their perspectives and are committed to finding suitable solutions.

Applying the Godly Principle - Patience and Grace: The Godly principle to apply in this step is patience and grace. Sales professionals can follow

Jesus' example of patient responses and extend grace to their customers, acknowledging their objections and seeking to address them with understanding and respect.

Example: Consider a salesperson selling a new software solution to a potential client. The client expresses concerns about the product's learning curve and compatibility with their existing systems. Instead of rushing to convince the client, the salesperson responds with patience, acknowledging the valid concerns. They offer to provide additional training and support to ease the learning process and address the client's compatibility questions by demonstrating the software's compatibility with similar systems used by other satisfied customers.

Benefits to the Customer: By applying the Godly principle of patience and grace, the salesperson creates an atmosphere of trust and openness. The customer feels heard and valued, knowing that their concerns are taken seriously. This approach fosters a collaborative and respectful relationship, allowing the customer to feel more comfortable with the purchasing decision.

Relevant Bible Verses:

1 Peter 3:15- *"But in your hearts revere Christ as Lord. Always be prepared to give an answer to everyone who asks you to give the reason for the hope that you have. But do this with gentleness and respect."*

Application of the Principle: Just as we are encouraged to give answers with gentleness and respect, sales professionals can approach objections with patience and grace. By demonstrating understanding and respect for the customer's concerns, we can foster a positive and fruitful conversation.

Conclusion: In removing objections and concerns, sales professionals can learn from Jesus' patient and gracious approach. Applying the Godly principle of patience and grace allows sales professionals to overcome resistance and build trust with their customers. By engaging in meaningful dialogue and addressing objections with understanding, sales professionals create a foundation for a trusting and lasting business relationship.

Selling Additional Items: Up-selling/Cross-selling-Negotiating and Closing with Jesus' Servant Leadership

The step of up-selling, cross-selling, negotiating, and closing requires delicacy and empathy. By adopting Jesus' servant leadership approach, sales professionals can prioritize the customers' needs and serve them with genuine care, rather than pursuing personal gain.

Jesus' Focus on Serving Others Rather Than Personal Gain: Throughout His ministry, Jesus consistently demonstrated servant leadership, putting the needs of others before His own. He taught His disciples to serve with humility and compassion, highlighting the importance of selflessness in serving the Kingdom of God. Jesus' ultimate act of servant leadership was His sacrificial death on the cross, symbolizing His love and service for humanity.

Applying Servant Leadership in Up-selling, Cross-selling, and Closing: Sales professionals can apply the Godly principle of servant leadership in up-selling, cross-selling, negotiating, and closing. Instead of solely aiming for higher sales and personal gain, they focus on understanding the customers' desires and needs. They offer additional products or services that genuinely enhance the customers' experience and meet their requirements, rather than pressuring them into unnecessary purchases.

Example: A salesperson is assisting a customer in purchasing a new laptop. After understanding the customer's needs and budget, the salesperson suggests a few additional accessories, such as a laptop bag and a wireless mouse, to improve the customer's convenience and productivity. The salesperson explains how these items complement the laptop's features and align with the customer's usage patterns, ensuring that the customer can make an informed decision.

Benefits to the Customer: By applying the Godly principle of servant leadership, the salesperson focuses on the customer's well-being and offers personalized solutions that genuinely enhance their experience. The customer feels valued and understood, knowing that the salesperson's recommendations are made with their best interests at heart. This approach fosters trust and loyalty, leading to a stronger and more fruitful relationship between the salesperson and the customer.

Relevant Bible Verses:

Mark 10:45 - *"For even the Son of Man did not come to be served, but to serve, and to give his life as a ransom for many."*

Application of the Principle: Just as Jesus came to serve and give His life for others, sales professionals can apply servant leadership in their interactions with customers. By prioritizing the customers' needs and offering genuine value, sales professionals can embody the spirit of service in their sales approach.

Conclusion: In up-selling, cross-selling, negotiating, and closing, sales professionals can draw inspiration from Jesus' servant leadership. Applying the Godly principle of putting others' interests before personal gain enables sales professionals to serve their customers with genuine care and empathy. By fostering a servant leadership mindset, sales professionals can create a meaningful and impactful sales experience that leads to customer satisfaction and loyalty.

Steps to Effectively Close Sales Deals using Godly Principles and the Model of Jesus

Effectively closing a sales deal using Godly principles and the model of Jesus involves fostering genuine relationships, understanding customer needs, and providing valuable solutions. Here are the steps and techniques, along with biblical examples and real-world applications:

1. **Active Listening and Empathy:** Listen attentively to the customer's needs and concerns, showing genuine empathy for their challenges and desires. Understand their pain points and aspirations.
   Biblical Example: Jesus' encounter with the blind beggar Bartimaeus (Mark 10:46-52). Jesus empathetically listened to Bartimaeus' plea for sight and restored his vision.
   Real-world Application: Engage customers in meaningful conversations, asking open-ended questions to understand their unique needs and motivations. Reflect their concerns and desires in your responses.
2. **Offer Tailored Solutions:** Based on the customer's needs, present customized solutions that address their specific challenges. Demonstrate how your product or service can add value to their lives.
   Biblical Example: Jesus' interaction with the woman at the well (John 4:1-42). Jesus addressed the Samaritan woman's thirst for

living water, offering her a transformative solution to her spiritual needs.
Real-world Application: Tailor your presentation to highlight the benefits most relevant to the customer. Show how your solution aligns with their goals and meets their requirements.

3. **Addressing Objections with Grace:** Anticipate and handle objections with patience and grace, addressing each concern thoughtfully without becoming defensive.
   Biblical Example: Jesus' response to the Pharisees' objections about healing on the Sabbath (Luke 14:1-6). Jesus handled their concerns with wisdom, highlighting the value of showing compassion on the Sabbath.
   Real-world Application: Acknowledge objections without downplaying or dismissing them. Provide clear explanations and supporting evidence to address concerns effectively.
4. **Using Testimonials and Social Proof:** Share success stories and testimonials from satisfied customers to build trust and credibility.
   Biblical Example: The testimony of the blind man healed by Jesus (John 9:1-41). The blind man's personal testimony became a powerful testament to the miraculous healing he received from Jesus.
   Real-world Application: Incorporate testimonials and case studies into your sales pitch to showcase the positive experiences of previous customers and demonstrate the value of your offering.

5. **Creating a Sense of Urgency:** Encourage timely action without resorting to pressure tactics. Show how acting promptly can lead to benefits or prevent potential challenges.
   Biblical Example: Jesus' call for immediate action in response to His teachings (Matthew 4:17-22). Jesus urged His disciples to repent and follow Him without delay.
   Real-world Application: Highlight limited-time offers, exclusive deals, or product availability to encourage customers to make a decision without feeling rushed.
6. **Seeking Agreement and Closing with Confidence:** Once objections are resolved and needs are addressed, seek agreement from the customer and confidently ask for the sale.
   Biblical Example: Jesus' invitation to Peter to become a fisher of men (Luke 5:1-11). After Jesus performed a miraculous catch of fish, He confidently invited Peter to join Him in His mission.
   Real-world Application: Ask closing questions that guide the customer toward a decision. Be confident and assured in your tone, showing that you believe in the value of your offering.
7. **Follow-Up and Relationship Building:** After the sale, maintain communication and build a lasting relationship with the customer. Express gratitude for their trust and offer ongoing support.
   Biblical Example: Jesus' post-resurrection appearance to the disciples (John 21:1-14). Jesus' continued presence and support

strengthened His disciples' faith and commitment.

Real-world Application: Send follow-up emails or make courtesy calls to express appreciation and inquire about their satisfaction. Stay connected to provide support and build trust for future opportunities.

By integrating these steps and techniques rooted in Godly principles and Jesus' example, the Sales Professional can effectively close a sales deal with authenticity, empathy, and purpose. This approach not only leads to successful sales outcomes but also fosters meaningful and lasting relationships with customers, reflecting the heart of Jesus in every transaction.

Customer Service and Retention: Faithfulness and Love - Jesus' Model

The final step of the sales process, customer service, and retention is about building lasting relationships with customers. By emulating Jesus' unwavering love and care for His followers, sales professionals can prioritize faithfulness and love in serving their customers, ensuring their satisfaction and loyalty.

Jesus' Unwavering Love and Care for His Followers: Throughout His ministry, Jesus demonstrated unparalleled love and care for His disciples and followers. He showed compassion, healed the sick, fed the hungry, and provided spiritual guidance and support. Jesus' love was not conditional but selfless and enduring, emphasizing the importance of faithfulness in relationships.

Emphasizing Customer Service and Retention with Faithfulness and Love: Sales professionals can apply the Godly principles of faithfulness and love in customer service and retention. Instead of viewing customers as one-time transactions, they prioritize building lasting connections and providing ongoing support. This involves promptly addressing customer inquiries, providing after-sales support, and staying engaged to ensure the customers' ongoing satisfaction.

Example: After purchasing a new appliance from a store, a customer encounters an issue with its functioning. The sales professional, embodying Jesus' model of faithfulness and love, promptly responds to the customer's call for assistance. They arrange for a technician to visit the customer's home, fix the issue, and offer additional guidance on optimizing the appliance's performance. The sales professional follows up with the customer a few days later to ensure everything is functioning smoothly and addresses any further concerns.

Benefits to the Customer: By applying the Godly principle of faithfulness and love, the sales professional demonstrates genuine care and concern for the customer's well-being. The customer feels valued and supported, knowing they can rely on the sales professional for ongoing assistance. This approach fosters trust and strengthens the relationship, leading to long-term customer satisfaction and loyalty.

Relevant Bible Verses:

Lamentations 3:22-23 - *"Because of the Lord's great love, we are not consumed, for his compassions never fail. They are new every morning; great is your faithfulness."*

Application of the Principle: Just as the Lord's compassions never fail and His faithfulness is great, sales professionals can apply faithfulness and love in their approach to customer service and retention. By consistently demonstrating care and support, they reflect the enduring love and faithfulness exemplified by Jesus.

Conclusion: In customer service and retention, sales professionals can learn from Jesus' model of faithfulness and love. By applying the Godly principles of genuine care and ongoing support, sales professionals build lasting relationships with their customers. Embracing a servant leadership mindset, they prioritize the customers' well-being, leading to customer satisfaction and loyalty in the long run.

Walking in His Steps - The Journey of a Godly Sales Professional

The conclusion of the book highlights the significance of following Jesus' example in every step of the sales process. It serves as a reminder of the key lessons learned from Jesus' life and teachings, inspiring sales professionals to walk in His footsteps in their sales journey.

Recapitulating the Key Lessons from Jesus' Example in Each Step: In this section, the book summarizes the important lessons drawn from Jesus' life and how they relate to each step of the sales process:

1. Prospecting and Lead Generation: Compassionate outreach, genuine care for diverse individuals.
2. Preparing and Planning: Diligence in prayerful preparation and wisdom for effective engagement.
3. Approaching the Customer: Love and respect, breaking barriers for meaningful connections.
4. Uncovering Needs and Pain: Compassion and empathy in understanding customers' struggles.
5. Proving Value: Honesty and integrity, building credibility and trust with customers.
6. Removing Objections/Concerns: Patience and grace, engaging in thoughtful dialogue to overcome resistance.
7. Additional Items – Up-selling/Cross-selling, Closing: Putting others' interests first, focusing on genuine value.

8. Customer Service and Retention: Faithfulness and love, prioritizing lasting relationships and ongoing support.

Inspiring Sales Professionals to Follow Jesus' Footsteps: This book inspires sales professionals to adopt the Godly principles exemplified by Jesus in their daily interactions with customers. It encourages them to embody servant leadership, practicing honesty, empathy, and selflessness to enhance the customer experience.

Example: The book includes real-life stories of sales professionals who have successfully implemented Godly principles in their sales journey. These stories demonstrate how following Jesus' example has positively impacted both their careers and the lives of their customers.

Benefits to the Customer: By walking in the footsteps of Jesus, sales professionals prioritize serving their customers with love, empathy, and integrity. This approach fosters deeper connections and trust, leading to more meaningful and lasting relationships. As a result, customers feel valued and appreciated, enjoying a positive sales experience that goes beyond transactional interactions.

Relevant Bible Verses:

1 John 2:6 - *"Whoever claims to live in him must live as Jesus did."*

Application of the Principle: Sales professionals can apply the Godly principle of living as Jesus did by embodying His teachings and example in their daily interactions. By integrating the principles of compassion, honesty, and selflessness into their sales journey, they honor God and create a positive impact on their customers' lives.

Conclusion: The conclusion of the book reiterates the importance of following Jesus' example in the sales journey. By integrating Godly principles into every step of the sales process, sales professionals can create a positive and transformative experience for their customers. Embracing the servant leadership mindset and applying the teachings of love, integrity, and empathy, sales professionals can make a meaningful difference in the lives of those they serve. The journey of a Godly sales professional is one guided by the footsteps of Jesus, enriching both the sales process and the lives of their customers.

How JESUS as the Key Example Demonstrated these 8 Steps during HIS Ministry on Earth

1. **Prospecting and Lead Generation:** Jesus demonstrated a compassionate outreach to diverse individuals, seeking to connect with people from all walks of life. He actively engaged in prospecting and lead generation by reaching out to individuals who needed His message of love, salvation, and redemption. Example: In Mark 2:13-17, Jesus approached Levi, a tax collector, and invited him to follow Him. Despite the social stigma attached to tax collectors, Jesus saw the potential in Levi and extended His hand of friendship. This act of prospecting led to Levi becoming one of Jesus' disciples and ultimately transforming his life.
2. **Preparing and Planning:** Jesus demonstrated diligence and wisdom in His preparation for ministry. He spent time in prayer and fasting to seek God's guidance before significant events in His ministry. Example: Before selecting His disciples, Jesus spent the whole night in prayer (Luke 6:12-16). This preparation allowed Him to make wise decisions and choose the right individuals to carry forward His message.
3. **Approaching the Customer:** Jesus' approach to customers exemplified love and respect. He broke cultural norms and societal barriers to connect with people, regardless of

their background or status. Jesus' mannerisms and demeanor showed genuine care for each individual He encountered. Example: In John 4:4-26, Jesus approached a Samaritan woman at a well. Jews and Samaritans had a history of animosity, but Jesus disregarded these divisions and engaged her in conversation. He treated her with respect and addressed her spiritual needs, resulting in her transformation and belief in Him.

4. **Uncovering Needs and Pain:** Jesus showed profound empathy in understanding people's needs and struggles. He listened to their concerns and offered healing and restoration to those in pain. Example: In Matthew 14:13-21, when Jesus saw a large crowd hungry and tired, He had compassion on them. He miraculously fed thousands of people with just five loaves of bread and two fish, meeting their physical and spiritual needs.
5. **Proving Value Handling:** Jesus upheld honesty and integrity in His teachings and interactions. He proved the value of His message through His actions, always aligning His words with His deeds. Example: In John 8:1-11, when the scribes and Pharisees brought a woman caught in adultery to Jesus, He showed value handling by defending her and offering forgiveness. He emphasized the importance of mercy and truthfulness, setting an example of how to handle challenging situations with integrity.
6. **Removing Objections/Concerns:** Jesus addressed objections and concerns with

patience and grace. He engaged in thoughtful dialogue, addressing doubts and misunderstandings with understanding. Example: In John 20:24-29, when Thomas doubted the resurrection, Jesus appeared to him and patiently invited Thomas to touch His wounds. He handled Thomas' doubts with grace and lovingly addressed his concerns, leading to Thomas' confession of faith.

7. **Additional Items – Up-selling/Cross-selling, Negotiating and Closing:** Jesus always put others' interests first and focused on genuine value. He prioritized meeting the spiritual needs of people rather than seeking personal gain. Example: In Mark 10:17-27, a rich young ruler approached Jesus, seeking eternal life. Jesus challenged him to give up his worldly possessions to follow Him. Though the young man left sorrowful, Jesus demonstrated the importance of prioritizing eternal treasures over worldly gain.
8. **Customer Service and Retention:** Jesus' love and faithfulness were evident in His commitment to His disciples and followers. He provided ongoing support, guidance, and care, fostering lasting relationships. Example: After His resurrection, Jesus appeared to His disciples multiple times, assuring them of His continued presence and empowering them for their mission (John 21:15-19). His faithfulness and love led to the disciples' unwavering commitment to spreading His message after His ascension.

In every step of the sales process, Jesus exemplified Godly principles through His actions and teachings.

By following His example, sales professionals can cultivate a customer-centric approach that seeks to serve and meet the needs of others genuinely.

When Faced with Turn-downs and Rejections, what can a Sales Person Using JESUS as the Role Model do to Ensure He is Constantly Motivated and High on Energy

As a Sales Professional using Jesus as the Role Model, facing turn downs and rejections can indeed be challenging. However, drawing inspiration from Jesus' teachings and examples can help the salesperson stay motivated and high on energy. Here are some steps with examples from the Bible:

- ✓ **Seek Strength in Prayer:** Follow Jesus' example of seeking strength in prayer during difficult times. Spending time in prayer can provide comfort and renewed energy to face challenges. Example: Before His crucifixion, Jesus went to the Garden of Gethsemane to pray, seeking strength from God in His moment of great anguish (Matthew 26:36-44).
- ✓ **Focus on the Greater Purpose:** Keep the greater purpose in mind, just as Jesus did when He prioritized His mission to spread God's love and truth. Example: When Jesus faced opposition and rejection in Nazareth, He reminded Himself of His purpose and continued to teach in other towns (Luke 4:16-30).
- ✓ **Learn from Setbacks:** Embrace setbacks as opportunities for growth and learning. Jesus used challenging situations to teach His disciples and to demonstrate valuable lessons. Example: When the disciples faced

difficulty in healing a boy with a demon, Jesus used it as a teaching moment to emphasize the importance of faith (Mark 9:14-29).

- ✓ **Find Encouragement in Scripture:** Turn to Scripture for encouragement and motivation. The Bible is filled with passages that uplift and inspire. Example: The Psalms are a rich source of comfort and motivation. Psalm 34:17-18 reminds us that God is near to the brokenhearted and saves those who are crushed in spirit.
- ✓ **Surround Yourself with Supportive Community:** Connect with like-minded individuals who can provide support and encouragement during challenging times. Example: Jesus surrounded Himself with His disciples, who not only learned from Him but also provided companionship and support throughout His ministry.
- ✓ **Celebrate Small Victories:** Acknowledge and celebrate even the small victories in your sales journey. Each success, no matter how small, is worth acknowledging. Example: Jesus rejoiced when the seventy-two disciples He sent out returned with reports of successful ministry (Luke 10:17-20).
- ✓ **Stay Focused on God's Promises:** Remember the promises of God and have faith in His plans for your life and work. Example: Jesus encouraged His disciples to have faith and trust in God's provision, knowing that He cares for them (Matthew 6:25-34).

By following these steps and drawing inspiration from Jesus' life and teachings, the Sales Professional can stay motivated, resilient, and high on energy, even in the face of rejections and challenges. Keeping a strong connection with God, learning from setbacks, and finding encouragement in the Bible can empower the salesperson to embrace their role as a witness to Christ-like values in their profession.

Conclusion

As we come to the end of this journey, we stand in awe of the timeless wisdom and profound impact of Jesus, the ultimate Role Model in Sales. Throughout this book, we have explored the eight essential steps of selling through the lens of biblical principles, and we have witnessed how Jesus' example sets a transformative standard for our profession.

Embracing the virtues of compassion, honesty, patience, and selflessness, we have discovered that selling is not just a transactional exchange but an opportunity to touch lives and make a lasting difference. By adopting the heart of Jesus in our approach, we transcend the boundaries of conventional sales and become agents of positive change.

We have learned that integrity and ethics are not optional but essential foundations for building trust with our customers. We have seen that empathy and understanding pave the way for uncovering true needs and providing genuine solutions.

In emulating Jesus' servant leadership, we have experienced the joy of serving others, putting their interests before our own. Up-selling and cross-selling are no longer mere profit-driven activities but opportunities to enhance our customers' experiences and add value to their lives.

In our commitment to customer service and retention, we have understood the power of faithfulness and love, building lasting relationships that go beyond a single transaction.

Selling like Jesus is not an easy path, and we may face challenges and rejections along the way. Yet, armed with the example of Jesus' resilience and unwavering faith, we find the strength to persevere and continue making a positive impact in our field.

Let us go forth from this journey, not as sales professionals seeking personal gain, but as disciples of Jesus, committed to spreading His love and light in every interaction we have. May our sales journey be a testament to God's grace and compassion, as we carry Jesus' teachings into every sphere of our lives.

Thank you for embarking on this transformative journey with us. Together, let us sell with integrity, empathy, and purpose, guided by the perfect Role Model - Jesus Christ. As we embrace His example in sales, we are not only changing the way we do business but changing lives for the better.

May God bless your sales journey abundantly, as you continue to Sell like Jesus.

About the Author 'GERARD ASSEY'

Gerard Assey is a Graduate in Economics, a PGD in Management (HRD) and holds a Doctorate in Leadership. Gerard holds several International Qualifications in Sales, Debt Collection, Training & Teaching, and is a 'Fellow' of the prestigious 'Institute of Sales & Marketing Management'-UK, a Certified NLP Practitioner, a 'Certified Trainer', an 'Accredited Management Teacher-Behavioral Sciences', a 'Certified Competency Facilitator', a 'Certified Management Consultant'- (the International credentials of a professional management consultant, awarded in accordance with global standards of the ICMCI); and a Certification from the University of Michigan in 'Successful Negotiation: Essential Strategies and Skills'

He is also a Member of the 'National Association of Sales Professionals' backed with several years experience in varied industries, both in India and Overseas. He also holds an 'Etiquette Consultant' Certification from the USA (by Sue Fox, Author of Best Seller: 'Business Etiquette for Dummies'. She has trained some of the top celebrities' world over). He was also a recipient of a scholarship for extensive training in Japan on 'Corporate Management for India'.

Gerard Assey is 'Founder & Chief Corporate Trainer' of the Group: **'Citius, Altius, Fortius Unlimited'**- an organization that **celebrated 20 years of Glorious Service** in 2021, focusing on 3 Core Competencies:

People. Performance. Profit; in functional areas of Sales & Marketing, HR & Organizational Development, covering Recruitment, Training & Consultancy!

Having managed organizations with large Sales Forces in India & Overseas, his specialization cover extensive areas of Sales Training (All levels - Presentation, Negotiation, Key/ Strategic Accounts Management & Managerial Skills for all sectors), Bid Proposal/ Capture Planning/ Management Trainings, Retail Sales, Customer Service & Customer Retention Programs, Training for Prevention & Collection of Debt, Self & Personal Development Programs (Time Management, Teamwork & Team Building, Business Etiquette & Personal Grooming, Leadership & Managerial Skills, People Management Skills, Train-the-Trainer etc), including preparation of Custom-designed Business Manuals for Internal (HR, Induction, and Sales etc) & External use (Instruction, User Manuals).

Gerard has successfully conducted over 5980 Trainings & Workshops (as of Sept '23) all across India, Middle East, Africa, Europe & S.E. Asia. Besides public programs conducted regularly, both in India & Overseas, he has some of the top names as clients whom he services from Single Owners to large Public & Government undertakings, covering all sectors, for their in-house needs.

His website: www.CollectionSkills.com is the only one in this part of the world to be featured in the 'Collections & Credit Risk Magazine-USA' under 'Who's Who in Training' and ranks TOP, along with other websites listed below on most search engines.

Gerard is author of 77 books already (Sept 2023),

A few of the business related books being:

1. Bite-sized Bits on Commonsense Management
2. Heart to Heart on Life's Principles'
3. How to become a Successful Manager
4. The Sales Professionals' Master Workbook of S.Y.S.T.E.M.S
5. The Professional Business Email Etiquette Handbook & Guide
6. The Professional Business Video-Conferencing Etiquette Handbook & Guide
7. Professional Presentation Skills
8. Exceptional Customer Service
9. Professional Tele-Marketing Skills
10. Professional Debt Collection Skills
11. The G.R.E.A.T. Sales & Service Workbook
12. Sales Training Advantage for Results (*The Ultimate Sales Training Manual to enable you stand out as a S.T.A.R.*)
13. CEO Daily Planner & Organizer
14. The Sales Professionals' Master Daily Planner
15. The Professional Debt Collector's Master Daily Planner
16. My Daily Planner & Organizer
17. MY EMERGENCY INFORMATION RECORD (Family Emergency & Peace of Mind Planner)
18. The Ultimate Therapist & Counselors Planner and Organizer
19. Building an Ethical Workplace
20. Managing Relationships at Work
21. Managing Business Meetings Effectively
22. Effective Delegation Skills
23. Goal Setting for Success
24. B2B Selling by Email
25. Professional Business Etiquette & Grooming

26. Dining Etiquette & Table Manners
27. Effective Networking Skills
28. Grooming, Etiquette & Manners for Teens, Young Adults & Future Leaders
29. Inter-Personal Skills
30. Get Ready, Get Hired!
31. Selling in a Recession
32. Effective Receivables Management in an Economic Downturn!
33. Real Estate & Property Sales Training
34. Credit Sales & Accounts Receivable Management
35. Selling Skills for Real Estate & Property Advisors
36. Take G.R.E.A.T. C.A.R.E!
37. Spa, Salon & Health Club Selling Skills
38. Selling Travel, Holiday & MICE Services
39. Selling Skills for Spa's, Salons & Health Clubs
40. Retailing in Salons & Spas
41. Selling Holiday, Vacation, Tours & Packages
42. The Power of Sales Referrals
43. Selling Luxury
44. Technical Selling Skills Financial Advisors Sales Training
45. Dealing with Burnout at Work
46. Monopolize Your Markets
47. Selling to Affluent Customers
48. Financial Selling Skills
49. *The Effective Manager's Guide: Key Skills to Thrive*
50. From Aspiring to Inspiring: A Guide for New Managers on the Rise
51. The Power of Focus
52. Selling with Integrity: Sell Like Jesus The Perfect Role Model!

Besides regularly contributing to business & trade journals, including international ones such as the 'Creative Training Techniques' and the 'Sales News' of the U.S.A, He is also a member of several prestigious bodies & trade associations, having participated in many Conferences & Workshops in India & Overseas.

Prior to his last assignment of leading & managing a large MNC as head, Gerard had a 3-year stint in the Middle East as a Consultant with a leading British Consultancy Firm.

As the past 'Official Country Representative' for the International Business Award- 'THE STEVIES'-(the business world's own Oscar) for about 4 years- he ensured a few Indian companies that qualify for the same every year!

Gerard can be contacted at:

Email: training@Sales-Training.in,training@CollectionSkills.com
Websites:

www.Sales-Training.in
www.EtiquetteWorks.in
www.CollectionSkills.com
www.RetailSalesTraining.in
www.SalesTrainingIndia.com
www.ManualPreparation.com
www.TrainingWithPuppets.com
www.FirstContactAcademy.com
www.SalesAndMarketingRecruiter.com

Our TRAININGS & BOOKS that can help your team

- ✓ **Sales Effectiveness**: Selling Skills for any Sector: Service/ Logistics/ FMCG Realty/ Insurance & Finance/ Media/ SPA's, Health Clubs & Salons/ Key Account Management, Effective Negotiation Skills/ Bid & Proposal Management Skills/ Retail Sales Training: Any Sector (Auto, Jewelry, Clothing, Luxury etc)
- ✓ **Customer Service Skills**-Complaints Handling & Customer Retention
- ✓ **Debt Prevention & Collection Skills**
- ✓ **Etiquette & Grooming**
- ✓ **Leadership & Managerial Skills**
- ✓ **Self & Personal Development Skills**: Presentation Skills/ Effective Communication Skills/Business Proposal Writing Skills/ Problem Solving & Decision Making Skills/ Empowering Secretaries-The perfect PA! (For Secretaries & PA's)/ Effective Time Management/ Teamwork & Teambuilding/ P.R.I.D.E- **P**ersonal **R**esponsibility **I**n **D**elivering **E**xcellence

A Few of Our Business Books
By the Top Corporate Trainer & Author of 77 Books! (Sep '23)
And...DAILY PLANNERS for Every Corporate Need!
All Books available Online on all leading Stores in E-book & Paperback Formats
Experts in Training for over 22 years:
Sales, Debt Prevention & Collection, Etiquette & Grooming,
Leadership & Managerial Skills, Self & Personal Development Programs
By the Top Corporate Trainer (Over 5980 workshops)
& Author of 77 Published Books (Sep'23)

www.ingramcontent.com/pod-product-compliance
Lightning Source LLC
LaVergne TN
LVHW050010180826
845678LV00021B/2520
9789392492822